Britain's Global Leadership

The positive future for a UK outside the EU

Ewen Stewart

The Bruges Group

The Bruges Group

First Published 2015
by The Bruges Group,
214 Linen Hall, 162-168 Regent Street, London W1B 5TB

Copyright © The Bruges Group 2015
http://www.brugesgroup.com/
www.brugesgroup.com
Bruges Group publications are not intended to represent a
corporate view of European and international developments.
Contributions are chosen on the basis of their intellectual
rigour and their ability to open up new avenues for debate.

Bretwalda Books
Unit 8, Fir Tree Close, Epsom,
Surrey KT17 3LD
info@BretwaldaBooks.com

ISBN 978-1-910440-40-7

Contents

About the Author

Ewen Stewart is Consulting Director of Global Britain. He read Economics and Politics at Aberdeen University and has worked in The City for over twenty-five years in fund management and equity strategy with major investment banks. He is the founding Director of Walbrook Economics which specialises in advising professional investors including institutions, hedge funds and wealth managers on their investment strategies. Ewen's work has been published extensively focusing on macro-economic and monetary policy, tax reform and Britain's relationship with Europe. Recent published work includes *Masking the Symptoms, a critique of QE* for the Centre of Policy Studies and for the TaxPayers' Alliance, *Stamp Duty – a counterproductive tax*. He has given lectures for, amongst others, the Institute of Economic Affairs and at Pembroke College, Cambridge on monetary policy. He is on the Management Council of the Freedom Association and on the Advisory Board of The Cobden Centre.

Executive Summary

- The Eurocentric orientation of the UK is misplaced. Emerging markets, by 2018 are expected to account for 45% of world GDP and the European Union's share will have declined from 34.1% to 20.2%, with the Eurozone representing an even smaller 14.6%. China's share is predicted to surpass the entire Eurozone by 2018.

- Nations that can address this extraordinary shift in global growth will capitalise most effectively with these new trade flows. The attractive European trade bloc, of the 1970's does not look so attractive in this light, given the Eurozone's inexorable decline of the share of global GDP. The UK is uniquely well placed to exploit these shifting trading patterns given its global links and its service and financial sector bias.

- Britain is uniquely positioned globally in terms of economic, cultural and soft and hard power assets. The UK is home to the worlds global language, the worlds most global city and many of the most notable global universities and research institutes. British legal ideas and the common law approach is admired the world over. It is the basis of a our stability. These advantages would continue irrespective of our membership of the EU.

- British manufacturing remains comfortably within the top ten, in terms of output, globally. The UK is now a net exporter of motor cars with four out of every five cars produced in Britain exported. Britain is the world's second most significant aerospace manufacturer, possesses two out of the top ten global pharmaceutical companies while also having strong positions in marine, defence systems, food, beverage and tobacco manufacture, off-shore engineering and high-end engineering and electronics. British design, be it in fashion or sports cars, continues to be world beating.

- Britain's manufacturing base has shrunk, in common with most other developed economies, as the Far East has undercut on price. However the UK retains a key skills base and has developed a high-end, high-margin capability. Membership of the EU, with its cost pressures has almost certainly done more harm than good to this capability. Industry has little to fear from withdrawal.

- The UK is a world leader in sport, media and culture. Higher education is also a great strength with British universities ranked amongst the best in the world. This coupled with the growing strength of the English language and our traditional excellent global links gives the UK real influence in world affairs. This will not change once we are outside the EU.

- While the US is the pre-eminent power accounting for 39% of all global defence expenditure and an even greater technological lead the UK's defence expenditure remains in the global top 4. Technologically too Britain's forces, while numerically modest, are highly advanced. Technology generally trumps numbers. The UK is perhaps one of only 5 or 6 nations that can still project power across the globe.

- As the worlds 5th largest economy Britain will not be isolated by leaving the EU. On the contrary British power would, in some cases, be enhanced. For example we would swap our 12% EU voting weight at the World Trade Organisation for a 100% British vote.

- The UK is currently estimated to be a member of 96 different international governmental organisations so the loss of one such organisation, albeit a very important one, is unlikely to be damaging.

- Inside the EU we are punching below our weight and should do better. Self-belief coupled with a hard analysis of the nexus of power and strategic advantage will lead to this being addressed but that can only be so once we are outside of the EU.

This paper is based on Ewen Stewart's speech to the Bruges Group's November 2014 conference. This publication could only have been written with the invaluable help and ideas of Ian Milne of Global Britain.

Introduction

Most people are, by nature, 'pro' the place they live. Few people do not want the best for Britain. While we may not all agree what is 'best' generally most peoples motives are honourable.

It is therefore intriguing until very recently, for two generations, or more, the majority view, in Parliament at least, has been that there was no real alternative to British membership of an 'ever closer union. They have stood silent as the EU has developed beyond all recognition since the UK joined in 1973. Many in Parliament, and indeed in senior levels of authority, must have been aware of the consequences of this namely that slowly, but steadily British independence would be eroded to the point where it was little more than an illusion with power residing predominantly in Brussels.

It is this author's conjecture that the foremost reason for this silent compliance was a wide held belief that Britain's 'best days were behind it' and that only by submerging the country into the EU could Britain have influence again. These individuals had convinced themselves that the UK was in inexorable decline. Thus by tagging on to a bigger entity could prosperity be regained.

This author believes this analysis has its origin in post-war thinking which might have had some credence in the troubled 1970's but simply misses the point today. This paper examines a number of key aspects of the British landscape trying to put our position in context examining aspects of the economy, finance, culture, soft and hard power.

The paper is not intended to be an exhaustive balance sheet list, nor some sort of chauvinistic 'we are best' tub thump, for while we do possess many strategic advantages I recognise that other nations also offer many valuable insights and ideas. However this is an opening shot at demonstrating that far from being in decline Britain remains an extraordinary creative and globally leading nation that still is a key player in many fields.

Those who believe Britain is in inexorable decline and there is no option but to pass over power to the European Union are wrong. They are yesterday's pessimists for the reality is, despite the constant knocking and lack of Westminster confidence the UK remains in an extraordinary strong and balanced global position. Those who would like to see Britain regain authority over its own affairs, but are afraid of their imagined consequences of so-called isolation, have in reality little to fear.

Part One

Language and Culture

The English Language – a key advantage

Beyond doubt English is becoming the global *lingua franca*. While English is only the third most widely spoken language globally, by native speakers, some way behind Mandarin and just behind Spanish, English is the only truly international language.

There are an estimated 365 million native speakers, representing around 5.5% of the global population. Estimates of how many have some working knowledge of the language vary, as definitions of competency are subjective. The Kryss Talaat survey suggests around 1 billion while the British council puts it at 1.5 billion. The CIA's estimate is even higher at 1.8 billion. By whatever measure is chosen English is easily the most understood language on the planet and is growing at a rate that far outstrips the others.

The chart at the top of the next page puts the top 20 languages in approximate numerical context. However not only is English the most widely understood language it is also the most widely distributed and embedded. The two following charts, using data from Weber, examine the number of countries where English and other key languages are widely spoken and also embedded into the legal process. Again the lead of English is substantial.

Not only has English established itself as the primary spoken language globally. But it's dominance is significantly more embedded than any of its rivals and not just where it is established legally. For example, according to Scopus, 80% of all scientific journals are indexed in English. Interestingly German was the predominant scientific language in the early part of the 20th century. Thus English hegemony is relatively recent and now almost total. It is hard to see a realistic challenge to this hegemony.

Number of Speakers by Language – Source: Ethnologue, Kryss Talaat and CIA

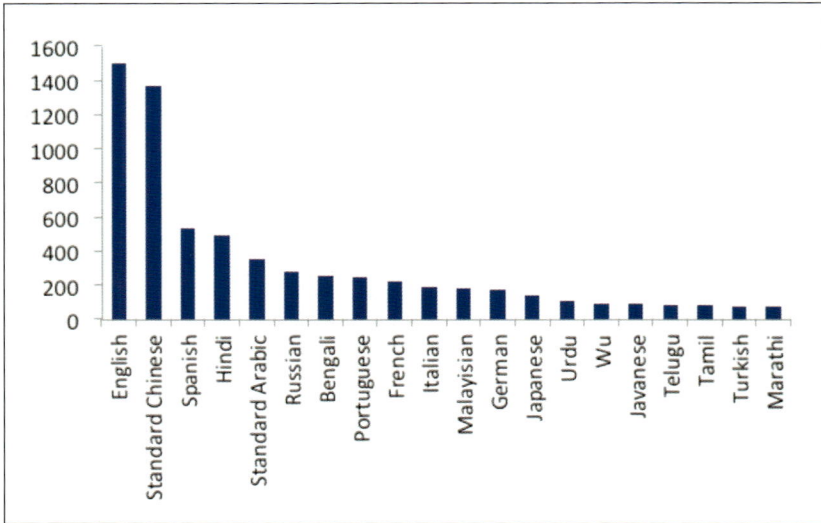

Number of Countries where a Language is Widely Spoken – Source: Weber

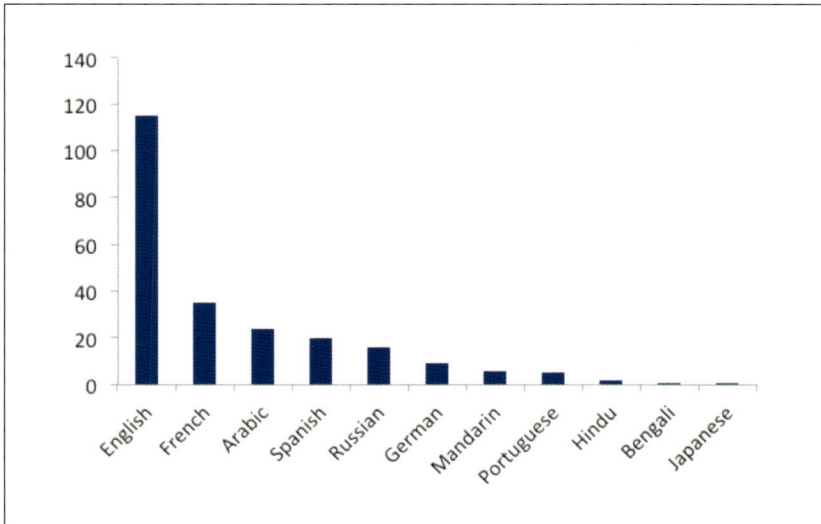

Number of Countries where the Language has Full Legal Status – Source: Weber

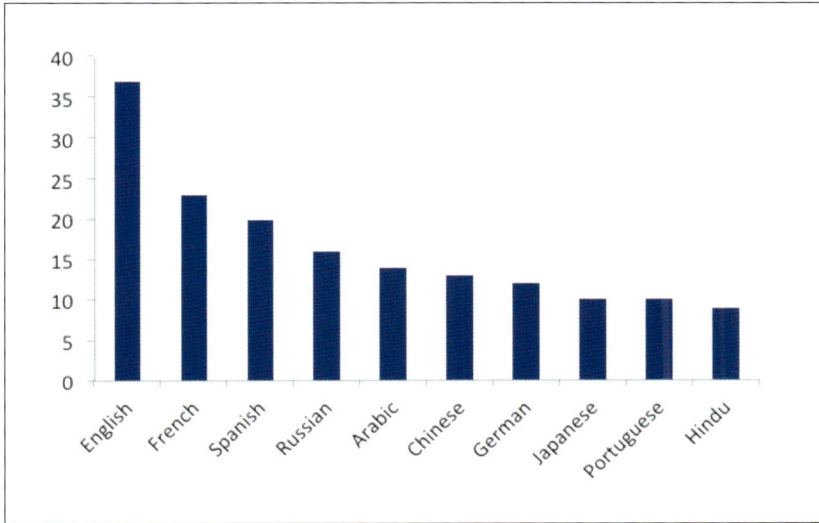

The Language of the Web – % of sites using language – Source: w3Techs

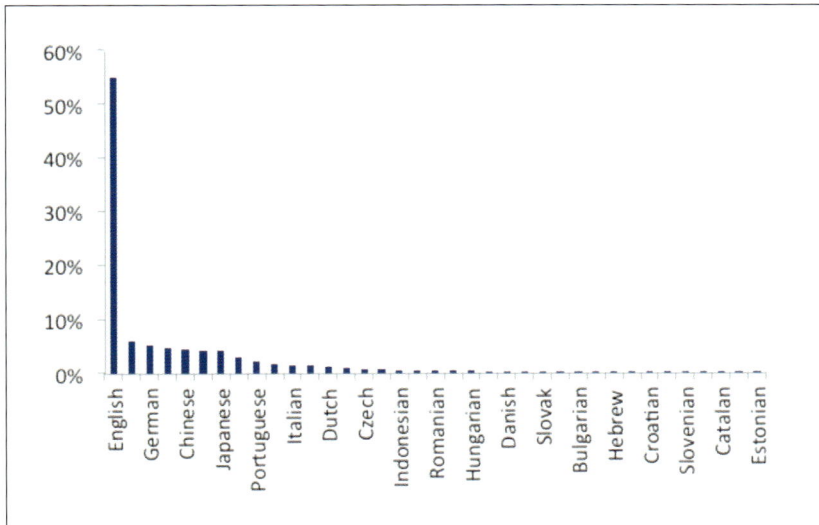

Further if we look at the new economy in the world wide web English is even more dominant relative to others. The last chart on the previous page underlines the ascendancy of English looking at the percentage of websites constructed by language. English has no serious challenger.

While historically the prevalence of language has ebbed and flowed, as empires have come and gone, it seems that in this first new global media and IT age 'first mover advantage' is key. English has that advantage and although some argue that the future is Mandarin and others Spanish once one language has become totally dominant as the preferred second tongue to the mother tongue in so many areas of society it is hard, in the view of this author, to see how it can be displaced.

While clearly Britain cannot take the full credit, if credit is the correct term, for the ascendancy of English (there are numerous factors behind English growth not least Hollywood and US power projection, as well as legacy from the British Empire, amongst others) we are in a uniquely fortunate position to be at the global centre of a language revolution. This advantage in terms of culture, ideas, business and trade is taken for granted but it is of enormous importance and value.

This position may have occurred partially by accident, partly through historical connections and partly down to US emergence as the global power but a great advantage it is. EU membership clearly has no bearing whatsoever on this boundless natural resource.

Education – a key strength at the Tertiary Level

It may not be entirely obvious, given the lamentable standards of much of the British state primary and secondary educational system but the UK is a global leader at the elite university level.

While comparing universities globally is fraught with difficulty *The Times* Annual University League Table is the established authority in ranking universities and it shows the dominance of the Anglo-sphere with a staggering 124 of the top 200 universities coming from the US, UK, Australia, Canada or New Zealand. Britain share, at 31, puts the UK in a clear second position in the global league table.

Top 200 Universities – Source: Times University League Table

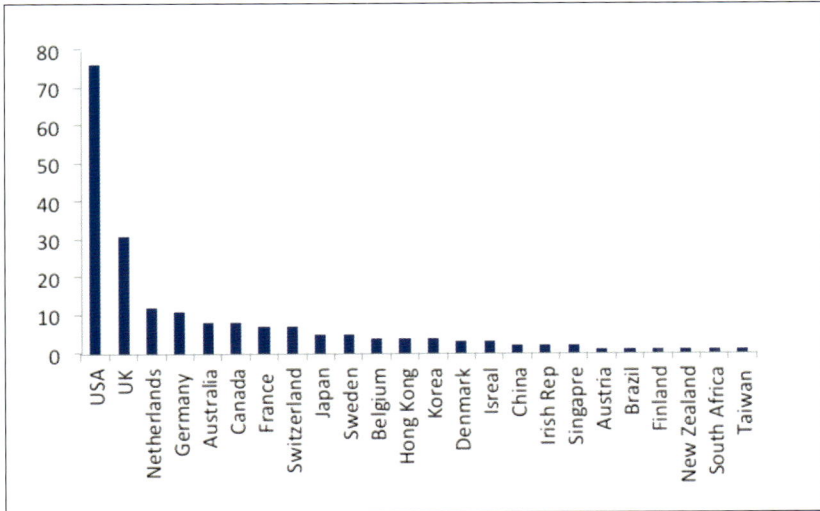

Not only that, at the pinnacle the UK has 6 out of the top 10 European universities. The entire eurozone can muster just one.

Top 10 European Universities – Source: Times University League Table

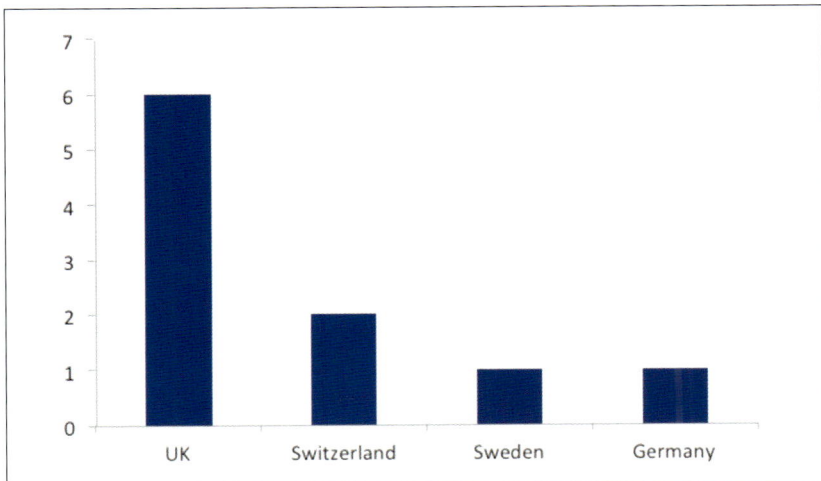

Further this is not just some declining historic advantage but a position that is strengthening. Of the world's top 100 universities under 50 years old 20 are British. At the tertiary level the UK is a clear global market leader and this would be unaffected by British withdrawal from the EU. In the 21st century thought leadership is critical and this is a key advantage we should nurture.

At the elite level Britain continues to perform at a level quite disproportionate to its population. The following chart shows one measure of this: the number of Nobel Laureates by nation and again the UK performance is highly credible.

Leadership in tertiary education, be it teaching, or research, is an immense 'knowledge based advantage almost beyond price. However a Department of Business Innovation and Skills report valued educational exports to be worth £17.5 billion in 2011up from £14.1billion in 2010. This is a market growing in excess of 10% per annum. This figure excludes benefits from patients and intellectual property rights and the like.
While there are significant problems and challenges with Government education policy the UK remains the clear European leader in tertiary education. This dominance would not be affected if the UK chose to leave the EU.

Number of Nobel Laureates by country – Source: Nobel Prize

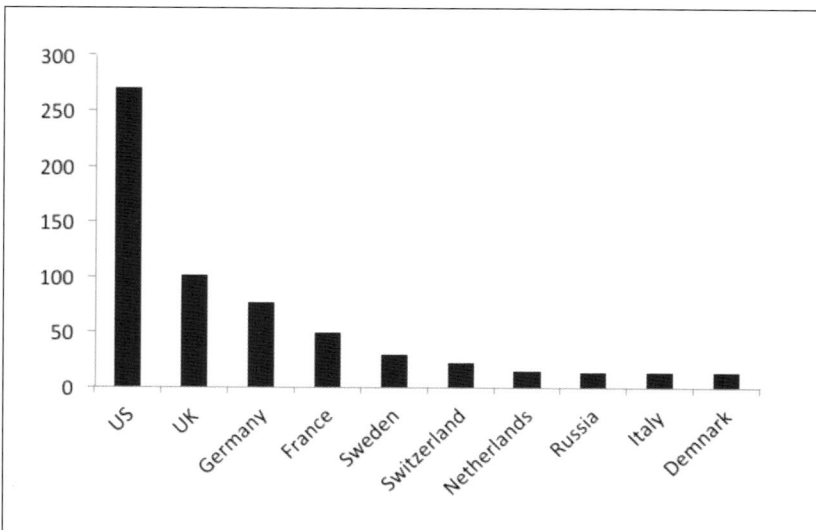

Sport, Culture and The Media – a leading position

While it would be futile and somewhat inappropriate to present 'a culture league table' few would argue that Britain offers one of the most varied and deep cultural environments.

While cultural excellence transcends national barriers and Europe, in general, has, for centuries, provided a deep well of creativity the UK's heritage remains a key advantage at both the elite and amateur level.

It was Edmund Burke who first drew attention to 'the little platoons' – those clubs and societies that took part in civic events as a uniquely strong British trait. Placing an economic value on such activities is futile but it is a key ingredient of an open and free society. What other country has so many diverse interest groups from the Royal Society for the Protection of Birds to the National Trust while founding OXFAM and Amnesty International for example.

Britain's heritage is renown (8th most visited tourist destination on earth), our galleries and museums and other national collections are amongst the deepest and most varied while the UK continues to host one of the richest veins of theatre and music (contemporary and classical) in the world.

In terms of media, while it may not be everyone's idea of the best way to organise television, the BBC arguably has the strongest brand name in the world and in some quarters still enjoys the perception of impartiality.

Sky TV also is a global leader and innovator in digital TV while the UK's reputation for creativity, drama and to some extent film remains strong. The English language advantage greatly aids our strategic advantage within this sphere.

Britain's press, although in decline, largely as a result of the growth of the internet, also remains at the forefront and as the press proved in the MP's expenses scandal, still has the ability to bring authority to account.

The UK's media services are also global leaders be it in advertising agencies, data providers like Thompson Reuters, professional and academic services through businesses for example Reed Elsevier or web information, design and services.

The UK's position in sport is also notable. England, may not have won the World Cup in recent memory but Britain's position as the sports capital of the world is extraordinary. It is borne from the ashes of the wealth of the industrial revolution as a leisured class enjoyed themselves. This country was the first to codify association football, rugby union and league, cricket, badminton, tennis, billiards, golf, bowls to name but a few.

Love it, or hate it, but the football Premier League is big business. It is a truly global brand transcending national boundaries. My brother was asked in Singapore, by a local, if he supported Manchester like him. The reply was no, Queen of the South. The English Premier League's (EPL's) revenues are the highest of any football league in the world at over £3 billion per year and the global TV rights are similarly significant. The brand also projects, for good or ill, British culture far and wide.

Britain is privileged to host, or co-host, a unique set of major sports at the highest level from the EPL, to cricket at Lords, grand slam tennis at Wimbledon, rugby at the Twickenham and Murrayfield and Cardiff Arms Park to the Open, The Grand National and Ascot, premier athletics, motor sport and rowing. The list is almost endless.

While a number of other European nations do host similarly prestigious events no other country can claim such a deep and diverse heritage hosting so many top events. This dominant position in hosting and organising elite sport across a number of fields has spawned a number of related industries where the UK also has leading exportable positions for example sports media, gambling and branded sportswear.

Indeed, Office for National Statistics (ONS) data demonstrated in 2012 creative industries in general accounted for 5.2% of the economy (£71.4 billion Gross Value Added) and provided 1.68 million jobs. The ONS figures suggested this area of the economy was growing at around 10% per annum. Britain's success, or otherwise, in sport and culture would remain independent of EU membership and remains a key strategic, albeit niche strength.

In conclusion while it is not possible to rank accurately Britain's sporting, cultural and media contribution few would argue against the proposition that it is market leading. The EU's role in this is at best negligible.

The Rule of Law, Corruption and Stability

We take it for granted but British society has been remarkably stable with a strong understanding and acceptance of the rule of law. This is a key and often ignored strength. Without attempting to recant a history of the rule of law from Magna Carta there is little doubt that British freedoms were won early and that subjects, under the Crown, so long as they lived within the law, could sleep easily at night.

Habeas Corpus was taken for granted until the introduction of the European Arrest Warrant, the supremacy of contract law and the avoidance of arbitrary justice embedded and the common sense approach of the Common Law, based on precedent, is perhaps the nation's greatest gift to the world. These advantages have been primary factors behind the prosperity this country enjoys. They are also a motivating factor behind the large number of people who seek to want to live here.

In the authors opinion these freedoms are under threat, albeit it the threat is relative compared with the position of many other nations. Remaining in the European Union is in our opinion one of the greatest threats to these freedoms as a new form of Law not based on the common law and precedent and, at best, loosely anchored in democratic legitimacy uproots our traditional freedoms. We are in little doubt leaving the EU would strengthen British law and justice by restating the supremacy of the Common Law and greatly increasing democratic accountability.

Coupled with the rule of law is stability. Britain has had its moments and battles. The 1970's Trade Union ascendancy being a recent one but few would argue that this country has been anything other than one of the most stable on earth for centuries. There is no reason to believe circumstance has changed and an independent Britain would not continue to be highly stable.

Britain may not be the least corrupt nation on earth, as measured by Transparency International, but despite much publicised problems with parliamentary sleaze the UK remains, in common with much of Northern Europe, the US and Old Commonwealth, a pretty transparent society. Sure there are problems but compared with large tracts of the world we continue to live without arbitrary rule.

In conclusion Britain, despite ever greater regulatory complexity and questionable short term legislation remains one of the most stable nations on earth. In the authors view this would be enhanced by exit from the EU.

Global Corruption Index 2014 – Source: Transparency international

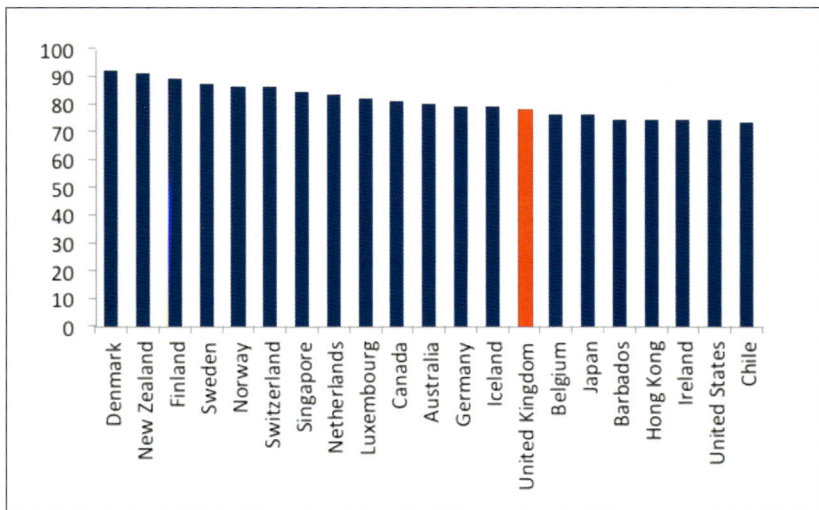

London – World's First Global Capital?

There are, in the author's opinion, really only two key contenders for the title Global Capital of the World. One is New York and the other London. While such judgements are clearly subjective those two cities combine a unique cocktail of economic, financial and cultural power and in the case of London political power too.

There are a number of surveys ranking global cities, and the results tend to be surprisingly similar. The AT Kearney survey 2014 results are highlighted in the next table. This survey is a broad one; looking at business activity, human capital, information exchange, cultural experience and political engagement.

Possessing a global capital is a key strategic advantage as it is a magnet for investment, cultural exchange and soft power. London's ascendancy, over the last 20 or 30 years, taking it back to its dominant 19th century position has been achieved completely in isolation to the EU and given the depth of London's assets it is hard to see it being eclipsed by any rival European City.

AT Kearney Global Cities Index 2014 – Source: AT Kearney

1	New York	6	Los Angeles	11	Brussels
2	London	7	Chicago	12	Seoul
3	Paris	8	Beijing	13	Toronto
4	Tokyo	9	Singapore	14	Sydney
5	Hong Kong	10	Washington	15	Madrid

Part Two

Economics, Trade and Finance

The Importance of Nations – Europe in steep relative decline

Given the UK's problems in the 1960's and 1970's of excessive union power, high inflation and perceived relative decline one can see, in retrospect, why some people argued that Britain should attach itself to a recovering Europe. Add into the mix 'never again,' after the War, the EEC, as then was, seemed the answer.

Indeed examining IMF data in 1980, the EU accounted for 34.1% of the global economy compared with 26% for the US and just 2.8% for all of Chinas 1 billion plus people. Then 'advanced economies' represented 76.4% of the GDP of the entire planet. The West was the only show in town. Indeed as recently as 2004 the developed world still accounted for 78% of GDP with China's 4.6% share still little more than a minor irritation.

The charts opposite show how quickly the weights of the economies have changed. Emerging markets, by 2018 are expected to account for 45% of world GDP and the European Union's share will have declined from 34.1% to 20.2%, with the Eurozone representing an even smaller 14.6%. China's share is predicted to surpass the entire Eurozone by 2018.

This is critical as nations that can address this extraordinary shift in global growth will capitalise most effectively with these new trade flows. The attractive European trade bloc, of the 1970's does not look so attractive in this light, given the Eurozone's inexorable decline of the share of global GDP.

However the UK is uniquely well placed to exploit these shifting trading patterns given its global links and its service and financial sector bias.

Share of Global GDP since 1980 (%, GDP US$ equalised) – Source: IMF

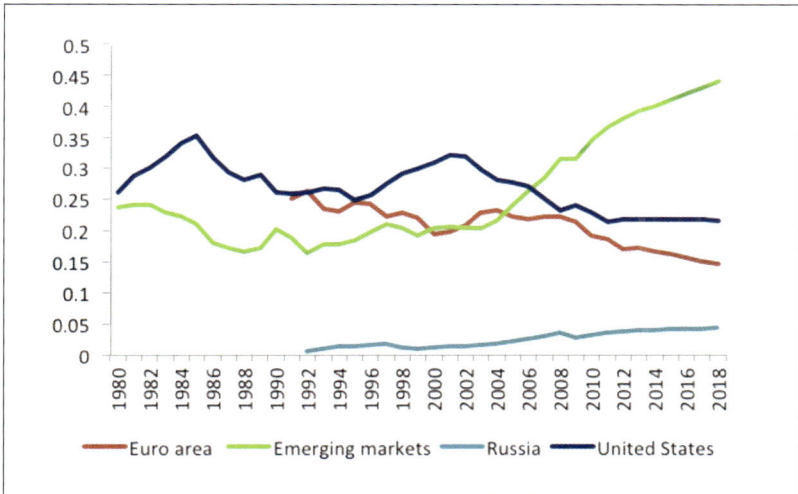

Share of Global GDP since 1980 (%, GDP US$ equalised) – Source: IMF

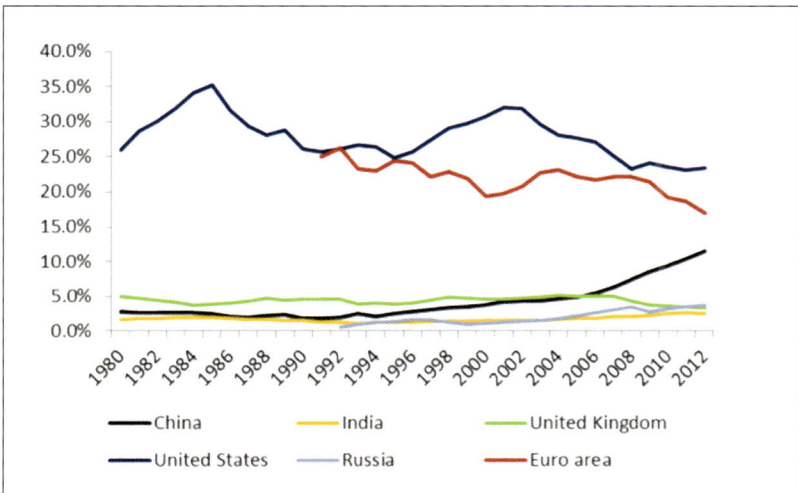

Trade – Changing Tides

Over the ten years from 2002 to 2012, British exports (of goods, services and income, transfers) to the rest of the EU grew at an average compound annual rate of 2.4%. Over that period, average UK inflation was at least 2.5% per annum. It follows that in "real" inflation-adjusted terms, British exports to the EU were lower in 2012 than in 2002.

The table below shows that "real" inflation-adjusted British exports to the "Big Four" EU continental countries – Germany, France, Italy and Spain – as well as to the Netherlands and Japan were all lower in 2012 than in 2002. With a couple of exceptions, positive (inflation-adjusted) British export growth came from outside Europe: the "BRICs" (Brazil, Russia, India, China and South Africa) the Anglosphere and Singapore, etc.

Export Market Growth 2000-2012 annual % change – Source: Blue Book and Global Britain

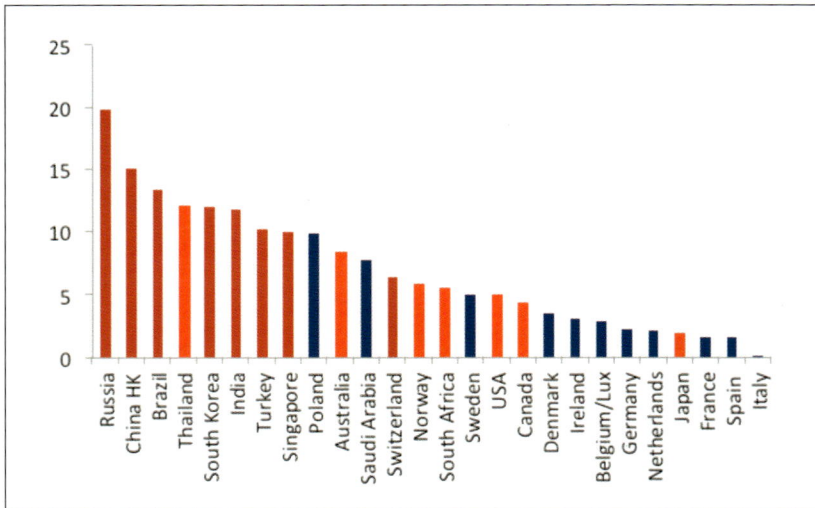

Over 2007-2012, the UK recorded a colossal balance of payments (i.e. "trade") deficit with the rest of the EU, and (except for 2008) a significant and growing surplus with the rest of the world.

UK Trade Balance EU and Rest of World £ billion 2007-2012 – Source: ONS

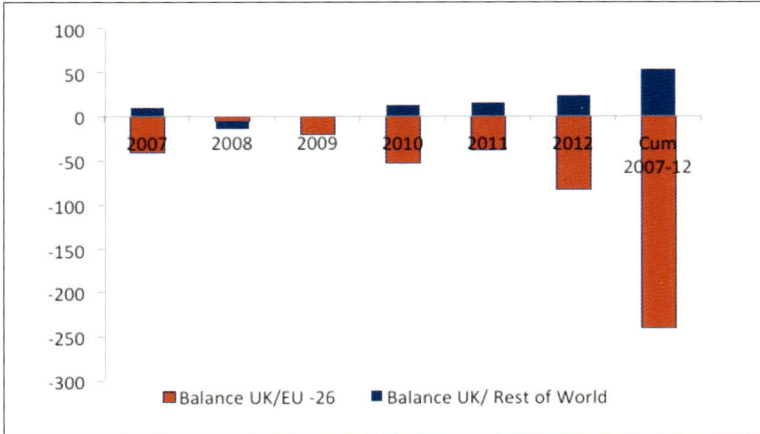

Projected Geographical Breakdown of UK Exports £ billion, EU, and Rest of the World
Source: ONS & Global Britain Estimates

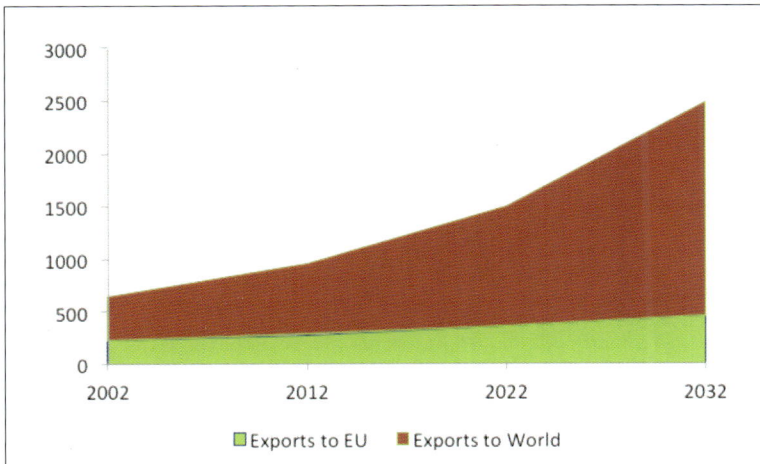

In 2012, the value of UK exports going outside the EU was 42% higher than the value of UK exports going to the EU. If, in future, UK exports to the EU and outside the EU grow at the same rate as between 2002 and 2012, the split in 2022 will be 69% to

non-EU, 31% to EU. Ten years later, in 2032, the split will be 78% to non-EU, 22% to EU.   Putting this another way: in 2022, the UK will be exporting more than twice as much outside the EU as to the EU, while in 2032, the UK will be exporting outside the UK three-and-a-half times as much outside the EU as to the EU.

High end engineering – still a workshop

In common with most Western economies manufacturing has shed a significant amount of labour over the last 30 or 40 years. Indeed according to the ONS 6.6 million people were engaged in manufacturing in the UK in 1978. Today that number has declined to around 2.6 million. However, although there has been a long term de-industrialisation in the UK, British manufacturing remains comfortably within the top, in terms of output, globally as can be seen from the chart below.

GVA of Manufacturing 2013 US $ million – Source: UN

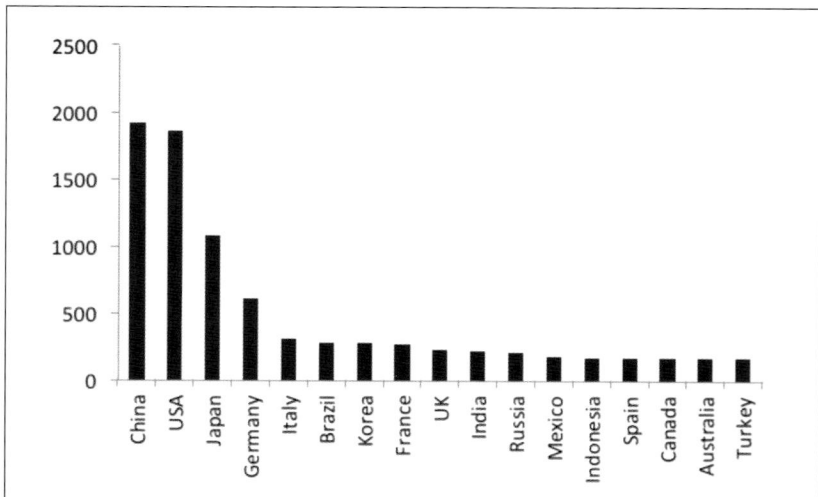

Given differential labour costs, between the West and emerging markets the UK's base is now generally categorised by being both niche and high margin thus creating a base where growth should be possible.

The UK is now a net exporter of motor cars with four out of every five cars produced in Britain exported. Britain is the world's second most significant aerospace manufacturer, possesses two out of the top ten global pharmaceutical companies while also having strong positions in marine, defence systems, food, beverage and tobacco manufacture, off-shore engineering and high-end engineering and electronics. British design, be it in fashion or sports cars, continues to be world beating.

In conclusion, Britain's manufacturing base has shrunk, in common with most other developed economies, as the Far East has undercut on price however the UK retains a key skills base and has developed a high-end, high-margin capability. Membership of the EU, with its regulatory and cost pressures has almost certainly done more harm than good to this capability. Industry has little to fear from withdrawal.

The City and Finance – clear leadership

According to the respected Zyen survey, which ranks the top global 79 financial centres by gauging their attractiveness both in absolute and dynamic terms Britain has the globe's leading centre, in London. What is more, from the Eurozone, only Frankfurt makes the top 10.

The Global Financial Centres Index 2013 – Source: Zyen Survey

1 London	5 Zurich	9 Seoul
2 New York	6 Tokyo	10 Frankfurt
3 Hong Kong	7 Geneva	11 Chicago
4 Singapore	8 Boston	

Further London's dominance was very broadly based leading in each of the 5 key competitiveness categories (people, business environment, market access, infrastructure and general competitiveness).

The financial sector, despite obvious problems in recent years, remains a key British jewel in what is a long term growth market. The sector accounts for around 10% of

British GDP and is estimated to have contributed £53 billion in tax receipts, out of the £549 billion raised in the 2011/12 financial year. This figure is almost certainly an underestimate due to the trickle-down effect 'The City' has on property, retail and other service trades.

Further, the financial sector generated a trade surplus of £44 billion in 2012, more significant than any other sector of the economy with 62% of that coming from outside the EU.

Britain's Trade Surplus in Financial Services 2012 – Source: ONSt

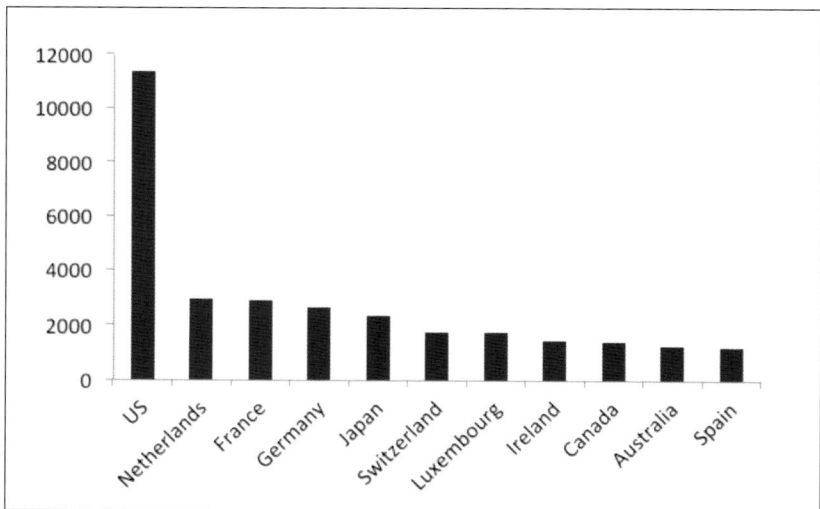

Britain's dominance in many sectors is quite extraordinary and totally disproportionate to the size of the UK economy. The following chart highlights global market shares in a number of key sectors.

Britain's Share of Global Financial Services – Source: The City UK

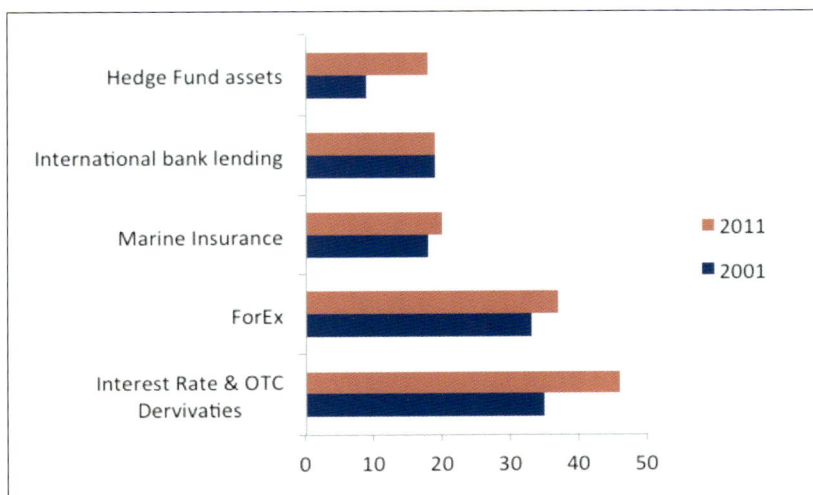

This dominance, in a European context is even starker as is demonstrated by the next chart. Ironically, despite euro enthusiasts arguing that British failure to join the single currency would be the death knell of 'the City' UK market shares have increased over the last decade in virtually all significant business lines. Of particular note is the UK's 74% of European foreign exchange trading which is all the more notable as the UK decided not to join the euro.

UK Share of European Financial Services 2012 – Source: The City UK

Interest Rates and OTC Derivative Trading	74
Foreign Exchange trading	74
Hedge Fund assets	85
Private Equity Funds Raised	42
Maritime Insurance Premiums	51
Pension Assets	49
Equity Market Capitalisation	37
Bank lending	17
UK Bank Assets	24
Insurance Premiums	18

Further as is demonstrated by the charts below Britain's portfolio of assets and liabilities is global with the European Union only accounting for around one third of assets. In a European context this is unique as our neighbours generally are much more interdependent.

UK Portfolio Investment Assets % – Source: IMF

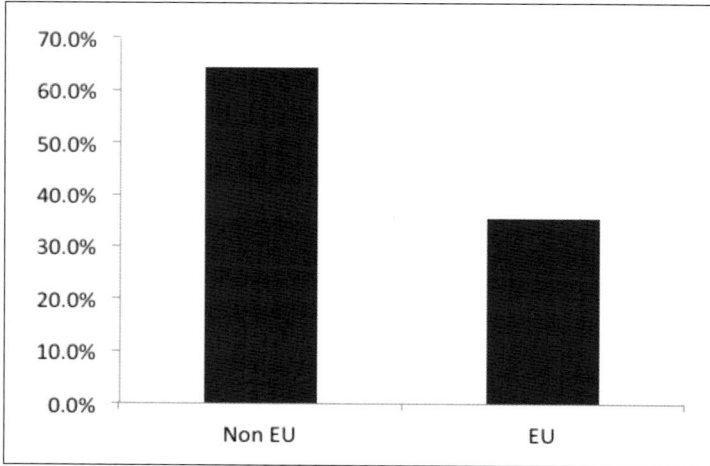

UK Portfolio Investment Liabilities % – Source: IMF

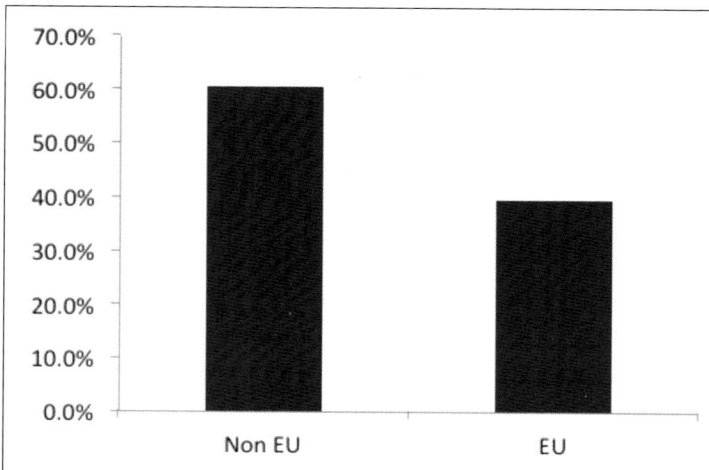

Currently there is no significant European Union country able to challenge the UK's dominant position in financial services. We believe a substantial challenge would be most unlikely to succeed from within the EU. The competitive advantage the City has developed in terms of skill sets, infrastructure, governance and connections makes an intra EU exodus most unlikely. Indeed financial services is to Britain what viniculture is to France.

This author is of the opinion that, despite the musings of some international investment banks, British withdrawal from the EU would actually cement Britain's dominant position not undermine it as regulation and policy would be directed domestically in contrast to the EU's somewhat heavy handed regulatory approach be it proposed transaction taxes, banking regulation or caps on salaries. The danger from continued British EU membership is that EU regulation drives business to other non EU centres like Zurich, Geneva or possibly the Far East.

The Financial Sector is simply too important to the UK economy and tax receipts to risk being regulated by a body whose traditions and interests do not necessarily match the free trade and open systems that the UK has adopted. There little doubt that the City would continue to dominate outside the European Union, just as it did, back in the 1920's, when Sterling ceased to be the world's global reserve currency.

IT – a surprising leader

When one thinks of IT one thinks of Silicon Valley and the likes of Apple and Microsoft. While it is true that Britain has not developed a company of that scale the UK is one of the worlds and on some measures, the most advanced, IT economy.

The UK is the global market leader in e-commerce. The next table puts this in context. UK consumers and businesses spend more than twice as much per head online as France or Germany and also significantly lead the US. Given the pace of global growth in e-commerce this leadership bodes well for future innovation and economic growth.

E-commerce Spend per head 2013 US $ – Source: ecommerce

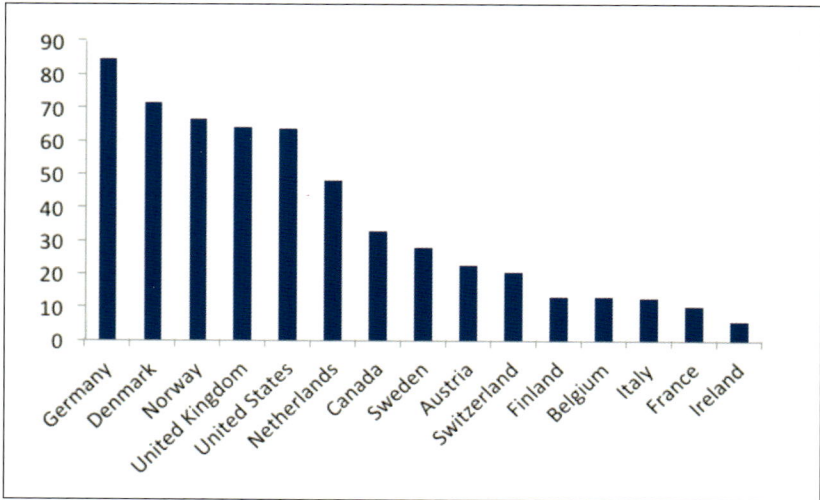

Further the UK has one of the strongest web positions globally as is seen from the chart below.

Number of websites per 1000 population – Source: Nation Master

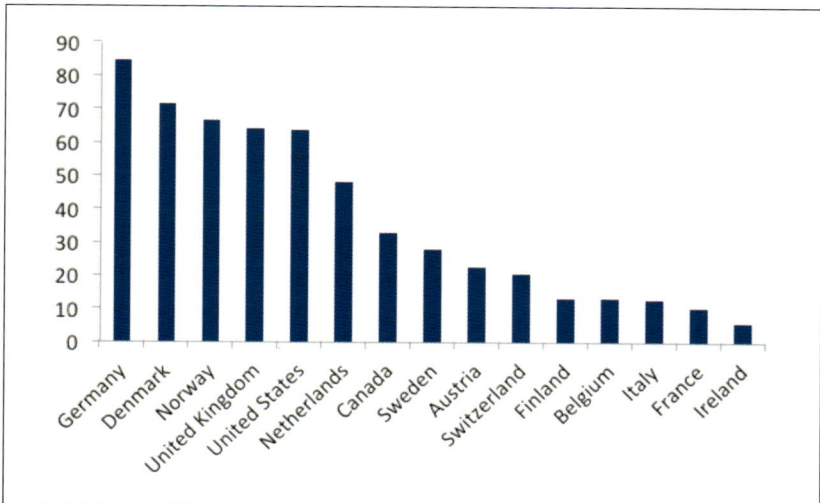

According to BrightHub, in 2013, with the exceptions of Hungary, Finland and the Czech Republic Britain's IT spend expressed as a proportion of GDP is the highest in the EU at 6.35%. German expenditure is a full percentage point lower at 5.3% with France at 5.1%. Again this bodes well for productivity and efficiency gains in the long term.

While the UK may have failed to develop major global software and hardware houses in its application we are a leader.

Natural Resources – a European leader

Britain has been geographically and geologically fortunate. Geographically due to a temperate, if somewhat disappointing climate, as an island which historically helped insulate the country from attack and by also encouraging trade and exploration.

And geologically through the ages with tin, then coal and now oil and gas and, in the future, potentially shale gas. Britain's oil production puts it just within the global top 20

Global Oil Production 2013 – Source: OPEC

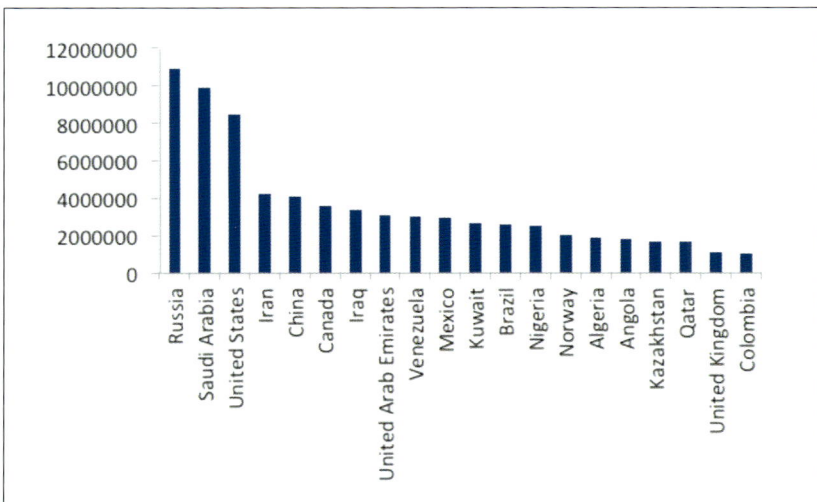

and the UK remains self-sufficient in oil. Although the North Sea Oil reserves are mature and production is in gradual decline the UK is likely to remain a significant oil producer for the next few decades. Despite the recent collapse in the oil price this remains a strategic strength unrelated to our EU membership.

However, if we put UK oil production in a European Union context the UK's share is greater than the other 26 countries put together. While Britain is just about self-sufficient in production an EU without the UK has a very serious deficit.

UK and European Union Oil Production 2013 – Source: OPEC

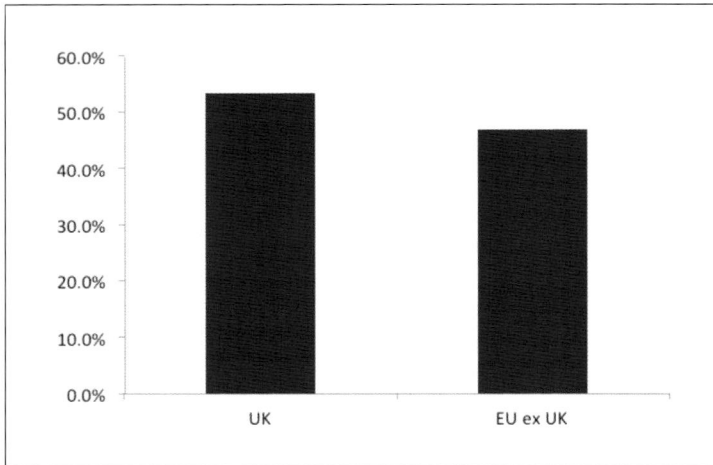

In terms of gas there are only two significant players in the EU – the Netherlands and the UK. Conventional British gas production is in decline, as the fields are mature, but the UK relative to the rest of the EU remains in a very strong position. EU, or no EU, we have little dependency on Russia for our supplies.

% of EU Gas Production 2013 – Source: OECD

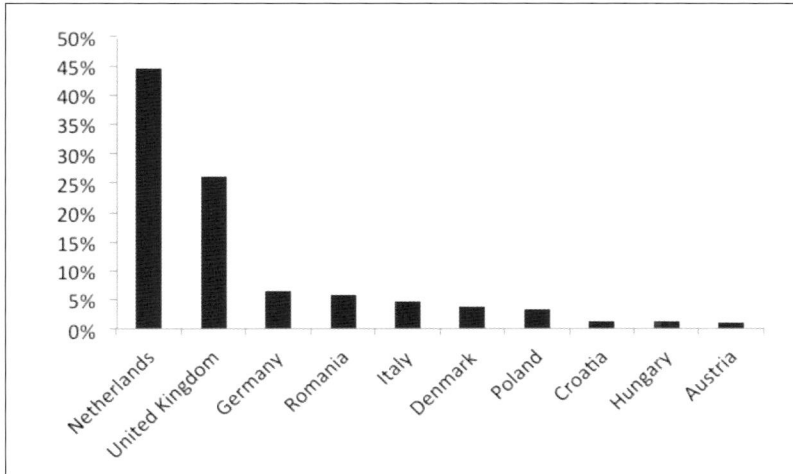

It is beyond the scope of this note to speculate about the impact of fracking. Certainly US gas prices are now one third of UK prices as fracking, in the US, has substantially changed the market. What can be said is the early geological surveys suggest that there is substantial potential in the UK, and elsewhere in Europe, to exploit this resource. Time will tell however, fracking, or no fracking, the UK is in easily the strongest position of any European nation in terms of carbon fuels. This fortunate position is also likely to continue for a generation or more.

Part Three

Power

Defence and Security – still a major force

Long gone are the days when the Royal Navy's supremacy was such that the fleet was larger than that of the second and third powers combined. However it is often underestimated how significant the UK's forces remain.

While the US is the preeminent power accounting for 39% of all global defence expenditure and an even greater technological lead the UK's defence expenditure remains in the global top 4. Technologically too Britain's forces, while numerically

Global Defence Expenditure US$ 2013 – Source: SIPRI

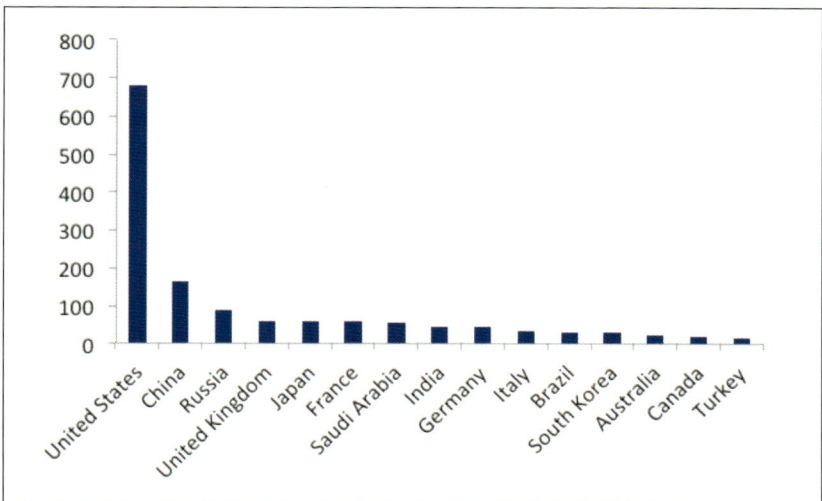

modest, are highly advanced. Technology generally trumps numbers. The UK is perhaps one of only 5 or 6 nations that can still project power across the globe.

In a European context the UK's position is even more significant and it is clear that the withdrawal from the EU would be a much more substantial problem for the EU than it would be for the UK, on defence and intelligence matters, as it would leave France as the sole substantial EU power.

European Military expenditure Euro's 2013 – Source: EuroStatt

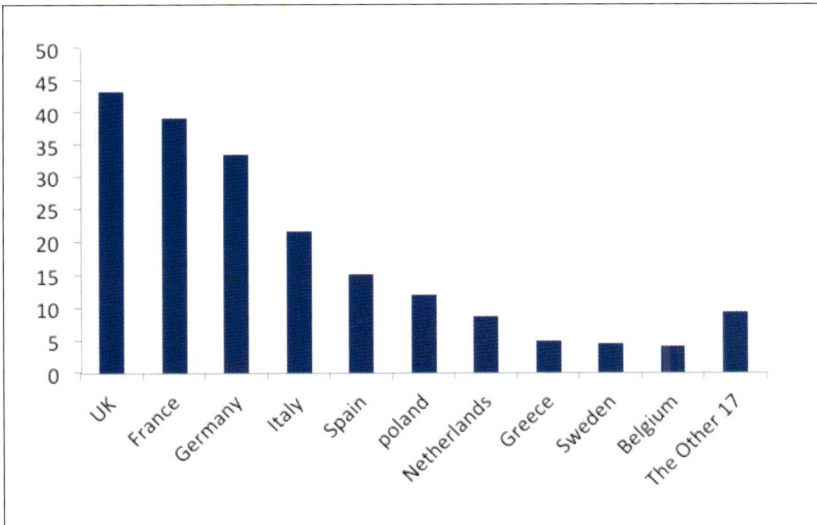

While one may question whether Britain has an adequately sized naval, air and land power the UK remains one of only a handful of nuclear armed nations and one of perhaps only 5 to possess sophisticated launch and range capabilities.

Nuclear Power-States – Source: CIA

US	France	Pakistan
Russia	China	North Korea
UK	India	Israel

Further the UK's forces remain particularly significant both in terms of strategic positioning with bases in Cyprus of particular importance given the instability of the Middle East. The UK's Special Forces and intelligence gathering networks also enhance power and remain amongst the strongest globally. British position as a Permanent Member of the Security Council coupled with a strong diplomatic tradition further enhances power.

The UK's special relationship with America may at times be a poisoned chalice but the harsh reality is the UK remains the only significant reliable ally to the world's only superpower, the USA. Such a position is likely to be close to US minds and should the UK leave the EU. It remains probable that the value of these assets (reliability, Special Forces, diplomacy through the Permanent Membership of the UN Security Council and intelligence sharing) will mean the UK's relationship with the US remains preeminent despite recent US comments.

International Organisations – quite a lot of Clubs

It is sometimes said that the UK would be isolated if she left the EU. The UK is currently estimated to be a member of 96 different international governmental organisations so the loss of one such organisation, albeit a very important one, is unlikely to be fatal.

We list the international memberships currently held. The most important ones, in our view, are in bold.

International Non-Governmental Organisations where the UK is a member – Source: ONS

African Development Bank (AfDB) (non regional member)
African Union/United Nations Hybrid Operation in Darfur (UNAMID)
Arctic Council (observer)
Asian Development Bank (ADB) (non regional member)
Australia Group
Bank for International Settlements (BIS)
British-Irish Council (BIC)
Caribbean Development Bank (CDB) (non regional member)

Commonwealth of Nations
Council of Europe (CE)
Council of the Baltic Sea States (CBSS)
Euro-Atlantic Partnership Council (EAPC)
European Bank for Reconstruction and Development (EBRD)
European Investment Bank (EIB)
European Organization for the Exploitation of Meteorological Satellites
  (EUMETSAT)
European Organization for Nuclear Research (CERN)
European Space Agency (ESA)
European Union (EU)
Food and Agriculture Organization (FAO)
General Conference on Weights and Measures (CGPM)
Group of Five (G5)
Group of Eight (G8)
Group of Ten (G10)
Group of Twenty Finance Ministers and Central Bank Governors (G20)
Inter-American Development Bank (IADB)
International Atomic Energy Agency (IAEA)
International Bank for Reconstruction and Development (IBRD)
International Chamber of Commerce (ICC)
International Civil Aviation Organization (ICAO)
International Confederation of Free Trade Unions (ICFTU)
International Criminal Court (ICCt)
International Criminal Police Organization – INTERPOL
International Development Association (IDA)
International Energy Agency (IEA)
International Federation of Red Cross and Red Crescent Societies (IFRCS)
International Finance Corporation (IFC)
International Fund for Agricultural Development (IFAD)
International Hydrographic Organization (IHO)
International Labour Organization (ILO)
International Maritime Organization (IMO)
International Mobile Satellite Organization (IMSO)
International Monetary Fund (IMF)
International Olympic Committee (IOC)

International Organization for Migration (IOM)
International Organization for Standardization (ISO)
International Red Cross and Red Crescent Movement (ICRM)
International Telecommunication Union (ITU)
International Telecommunications Satellite Organization (ITSO)
Inter-Parliamentary Union (IPU)
Multilateral Investment Guarantee Agency (MIGA)
Non-Aligned Movement (NAM) (guest)
North Atlantic Treaty Organization (NATO)
Nuclear Energy Agency (NEA)
Nuclear Suppliers Group (NSG)
Organisation for Economic Co-operation and Development (OECD)
Organisation for the Prohibition of Chemical Weapons (OPCW)
Organization for Security and Co-operation in Europe (OSCE)
Organization of American States (OAS) (observer)
Pacific Islands Forum (PIF) (partner)
Paris Club
Permanent Court of Arbitration (PCA)
Secretariat of the Pacific Community (SPC)
Southeast European Cooperative Initiative (SECI) (observer)
United Nations (UN)
United Nations Conference on Trade and Development (UNCTAD)
United Nations Economic and Social Commission for Asia and the Pacific
    (UNESCAP)
United Nations Economic Commission for Africa (UNECA) (associate)
United Nations Economic Commission for Europe (UNECE)
United Nations Economic Commission for Latin America and the Caribbean
    (UNECLAC)
United Nations Educational, Scientific and Cultural Organization (UNESCO)
United Nations High Commissioner for Refugees (UNHCR)
United Nations Industrial Development Organization (UNIDO)
United Nations Interim Administration Mission in Kosovo (UNMIK)
United Nations Iraq-Kuwait Observation Mission (UNIKOM)
United Nations Mission in Bosnia and Herzegovina (UNMIBH)
United Nations Mission in Liberia (UNMIL)
United Nations Mission in Sierra Leone (UNAMSIL)

United Nations Mission in the Democratic Republic of Congo (MONUC)
United Nations Mission in the Sudan (UNMIS)
United Nations Observer Mission in Georgia (UNOMIG)
United Nations Peacekeeping Force in Cyprus (UNFICYP)
United Nations Relief and Works Agency for Palestine Refugees in the
  Near East (UNRWA)
United Nations Security Council (UNSC) (permanent member)
United Nations Transitional Administration in East Timor (UNTAET)
United Nations University (UNU)
Universal Postal Union (UPU)
Western European Union (WEU)
World Confederation of Labour (WCL)
World Customs Organization (WCO)
World Federation of Trade Unions (WFTU)
World Health Organization (WHO)
World Intellectual Property Organization (WIPO)
World Meteorological Organization (WMO)
World Tourism Organization (UNWTO)
World Trade Organization (WTO)
Zangger Committee (ZC)

Many of the above organisations may serve a dubious purpose however it is clear that an independent Britain would not be isolated. Far from it. Further British power in certain organisations may even be enhanced. For example our approximate 10% share of influence in the EU over its vote at the World Trade Organisation would become a 100% British vote. We conclude that Britain would be far from isolated outside the EU.

Soft Power is substantial

If power is about the ability to influence the behaviour of others to get the outcome you want there are a number of ways to achieve this end. Pleading probably won't work, but the barrel of a gun might. However in an age where such coercion is used only in extreme circumstances soft power comes in to play.

Soft power can be described as the ability to attract and co-opt rather than coerce, use force or give money as a means of persuasion It includes international perception, global media reach, inventions, education, diplomacy, the charity sector, culture, sport and architecture and international events and such like.

While measuring a countries influence, in these matters, is clearly subjective the Monacle Survey is viewed as the most reliable authority. Britain, in 2012, came first. Given the economic dominance of the USA and its cultural hegemony, via Hollywood, Apple and hamburgers this is an extraordinary feat. Last year the UK was second, behind Germany,

Britain's membership of the EU is again largely distinct from the UK's soft power hence British withdrawal should not influence this critical standing.

The Monocle 2013 Soft power Index – Source: Monocle

1	Germany	6	Sweden
2	United Kingdom	7	Australia
3	US	8	Switzerland
4	France	9	Canada
5	Japan	10	Italy

Conclusion

Themes and ideas can take generations to come to fruition. In our view a key driving force behind British engagement with the European Union has been a deep seated belief, post the loss of Empire that the UK was a power in decline and only by merging into a larger entity could influence be regained. Couple with undoubted economic difficulties, notably in the 1970's and a desire for 'never again' after two unimaginably destructive European conflicts in the 20th century the thinking behind the UK joining the EEC was understandable.

However times change. This research, examining a wide, but not exhaustive, series of national themes around three principal areas of culture, economics, trade and finance and power draws the firm conclusion that Britain remains in an extraordinarily strong global position and far from needing Europe, Europe actually needs Britain.

It is time to reassess Britain's relationship with Europe. The drivers behind our membership in the 1970's no longer hold. The EU, as a share of global trade and GDP is inexorable decline. The Eurozone itself will account for just 14.6% of global GDP by 2018.

Britain's soft power is increasing, not diminishing. The advantages of possessing the worlds mother tongue, stability and rule of law, the common law, the world's first truly global city and first rank cultural, media and sporting amenities places the UK in an unique position.

The UK's hard power is also often underestimated remaining one of a handful of blue water forces coupled with strong diplomatic, intelligence and Special Forces.

Economically the UK is in a far stronger position that most of the Eurozone. Britain dominates financial services, which despite problems, remains a key growth market, the manufacturing base, while diminished, tends to be high margin and niche and is still well within the global top 10. Specialisations tend to be in growth markets. Business and professional services are other key areas of expertise as are creativity and cultural assets. This too is a fast growing area with high barriers to entry. Our knowledge base is second only to America as witnessed by the dominance of Anglo-Saxon universities.

Ironically so embedded is the idea of decline in the national psyche that many of these advantages are overlooked. Douglas Hurd once said the 'UK punches above its weight.' This author thinks he got it the wrong way round. We are punching below our weight and should do better. Self-belief coupled with a hard analysis of the nexus of power and strategic advantage will lead to this being addressed but that can only be so once we are outside of the EU.